Original title:
Petal by Petal

Copyright © 2025 Creative Arts Management OÜ
All rights reserved.

Author: Dante Kingsley
ISBN HARDBACK: 978-1-80581-798-7
ISBN PAPERBACK: 978-1-80581-325-5
ISBN EBOOK: 978-1-80581-798-7

A Journey Through Color

In the garden, colors clash,
Red screams loud, while blue is brash.
Yellow giggles in the sun,
Green rolls eyes, but still has fun.

Purple struts, a royal sight,
Orange juggles, what a delight.
Pink is shy, peeks from behind,
But all agree, they're intertwined.

Unveiling Nature's Mysteries

Bees in bowties, buzzing cheer,
Whisper secrets, lend an ear.
The daffodils don't wear a frown,
They dance and twirl in pollen gowns.

Squirrels debate, nuts in hand,
While rabbits plot to form a band.
Nature's quirks, a comic show,
With laughs that make the flowers grow.

The Art of Fragility

A flower sneezes, petals drop,
They giggle, then rise up, non-stop.
With every breeze, they spin and twirl,
A soft ballet, a floral whirl.

Butterflies sport polka dots,
As ladybugs play silly slots.
In fragile realms, the laughter's loud,
Each bloom appears, so silly, proud.

Shades of Silence

In muted hues, the world winks bright,
A quiet joke in the moonlight.
Grasses giggle, swaying so light,
As shadows dance, ready for flight.

Moss wraps secrets, soft and neat,
While crickets pull a midnight feat.
In silence shared, the fun unfolds,
Where whispers of humor gently hold.

Echoes of Springing Life

A flower sneezed, what a sight,
Pollen flew with all its might.
The bees all buzzed, oh what a show,
Laughing loudly, they stole the glow.

Bright green shoots stick out like thumbs,
Chirping birds, their silly drums.
A dance-off between the blooms,
Springtime humor fills the rooms.

Secrets in Each Blossom

Whispers hidden among the leaves,
Squirrels plotting heists in sleeves.
A daffodil winks at the sun,
'Catch me later, I'm not done!'

Tulips boasting, 'Look at me!'
'Oh no, you did not just see!'
They sway and dip with cheeky glee,
Nature's jesters, wild and free.

Touching the Velvet Hues

Velvet petals soft as dreams,
A rose that giggles, or so it seems.
Colors clash in a playful fight,
Who wore it best? It's a delight!

Daisies chatter, a blooming crew,
"Hey, I wore that!" "No, it's mine too!"
They swap their hues like fashion tips,
Each bloom laughing 'til it tips.

Gentle Reminders of Growth

A tiny sprout with lofty goals,
Dreams of greatness in its rolls.
It stretches up, but wait, zonked!
A bug climbs up, it's quite the honk!

Nature giggles at the sight,
A snail races in its flight,
A tumble here, a flopping there,
Growth can be quite the wild affair!

Beyond the Surface

Underneath the sunny gloom,
A frog thinks he's a flower's bloom.
He croaks a tune, quite out of rhyme,
And sprinkles skies with stolen thyme.

A snail on roller skates goes by,
With hopes to catch a butterfly.
He glides along, his eyes aglow,
As daisies giggle, waving slow.

A Whisper Amongst the Leaves

The squirrels gossip on a branch,
About the flowers' springtime dance.
They toss acorns, laughter swells,
As petals blush with their own spells.

A breeze jogs past, it starts to tease,
The flowers nod and dance with ease.
They play hide and seek with the sun,
And giggle when the day is done.

Tracing Soft Edges

A bumblebee with big plans spins,
Around the blooms, where laughter begins.
He trips on pollen, oh what a sight,
As tulips chuckle soft and light.

A worm on stilts, he tips and sways,
Content to dance through rainy days.
He twirls and wriggles without a care,
His friends all cheer, a wiggly air!

Nature's Gentle Revelation

Ants march along their busy path,
Plotting sweet tricks and harmless wrath.
A daisy snores, then wakes with a start,
"Oh dear, did I miss the garden's art?"

A lizard laughs, donning shades so cool,
He lounges back, his favorite pool.
With petals swirling in the breeze,
He smiles at life, and all with ease.

The Quiet Arrival of Beauty

A blossom skips, it twirls and leaps,
Wearing a smile while the gardener sleeps.
With its friends, it shares a jest,
"Who knew being pretty could be such a fest?"

The daisies laugh, the roses tease,
While the violets giggle in the breeze.
"Here comes the sun, let's all get dressed!"
In the garden party, they're feeling blessed.

Fading Into the Light

A sunflower sways, it tells a tale,
Of a bee that danced like a clumsy snail.
With every flinch, it trips and tumbles,
Creating laughter as the flower fumbles.

The night creeps in, the petals snore,
As moonbeams sneak in to steal the floor.
"Goodnight, dear friends, we've had our show!"
A gentle yawn, then off they go.

The Symphony of Soft Colors

A rainbow blooms in a vibrant row,
Each color plays, putting on a show.
The purples giggle, the yellows sing,
As the blues do the cha-cha, oh what a fling!

The orange glows and throws confetti,
While pink is twirling, looking all pretty.
"Join the fun! Don't be shy,
Let's raise a ruckus, let's all get high!"

Awakening the Silent Palette

In a canvas dark, there's a ruckus near,
Where brushes chat, and colors cheer.
"Let's wake the shades! Let's paint the day!"
Said one little splash with a bright bouquet.

The cobalt chuckles, the crimson winks,
As the silent palette suddenly thinks.
"Oh, what a sight! This will be grand,
Let's create laughter, isn't it planned?"

Layered Tenderness

A flower once wore a fancy hat,
It tipped to the side, oh what of that!
Bees laughed aloud, called it a clown,
As petals fell softly, it tumbled down.

The stem stood tall, but lost all its grace,
"Hold on!" it cried, "this isn't my place!"
A ladybug waltzed with elegant flair,
While daisies chuckled, with nary a care.

Tracing the Veins of Beauty

A leaf claimed to be the best in the park,
"I'm greener than you!" it sounded quite stark.
The rose rolled its eyes, said, "Really, how rude,
You're making the tulips feel quite misconstrued."

A squirrel stopped by, threw acorns with glee,
"Nature's best?" he mocked—"Let's wait and just see!"
While petals and leaves danced in the breeze,
They all shared a laugh, such joyous unease.

Soft Embrace of Flora

The violets whispered a secret so sweet,
About how to dance with the sun and the heat.
A sunflower giggled, its face to the sky,
"Come join my party, just don't be shy!"

A bumblebee buzzed with a jolly old tune,
"Let's party all night; I hope there's a moon!"
A shy little bud peeked out, and then blushed,
"Do you think I'm pretty, or am I too crushed?"

Nature's Subtle Flourish

A cactus wore sneakers, thought it was cool,
Said to the fern, "I'm no garden fool!"
The fern just chuckled, said, "That's quite a feat,
But how do you dance? You can't move your feet!"

A daisy chimed in, "Join my silly dance,
We'll twirl and we'll whirl, give nature a chance!"
And so, in the garden, they all started to play,
With laughter and sunshine, how bright was that day!

Uncovering Nature's Secrets

In the garden full of quirks,
The flowers hide in shady lurks.
A daisy plans a prank or two,
While sunflowers gossip, oh so blue.

A bee in shades of polka dots,
Sips nectar from the cozy pots.
Tulips wear their fancier hats,
As sneaky ants hold secret chats.

Foxgloves dance in the gentle breeze,
While daisies play pretend with ease.
Nature's secrets, funny and sly,
Make us chuckle, oh my oh my!

The Pathway to Fragrance

There's a trail of scents so sweet,
A whiff of cookies at my feet.
Lilies giggle, oh what a tease,
Like they know all the best recipes!

Roses blush in lovely hues,
While violets wear their favorite shoes.
Dandelions blow wishes to stars,
Hoping to travel in scented cars.

Jasmine whispers in the night,
With a scent that's pure delight.
Each step brings a laugh or grumble,
On this fragrant path, we tumble.

A Tapestry of Colors

In the field, a paint splash waits,
With shades that dance and giggle, mates.
Pinks and yellows, reds all around,
Each bloom thinking it's the most profound.

A clump of violets starts a race,
While marigolds keep up the pace.
With petals swaying, it's like a show,
Who knew the garden had a flow?

The palette shifts with morning's light,
Nature's rainbow, pure delight.
A tapestry of colors so bright,
Makes our hearts skip, what a sight!

When Silence Blooms

In the quiet, you might hear,
Petals giggle, spreading cheer.
A rose winks with a silly twist,
As tulips dance in morning mist.

Butterflies wear their finest gear,
Flapping wings in jest, oh dear!
The daisies chuckle, sharing jokes,
While thistles tickle, sneaky pokes.

When silence blooms in nature's space,
Laughter hides with quiet grace.
Among the leaves and whispers low,
A party starts, oh what a show!

Delicate Revelations

In the garden, a sneeze so loud,
Little buds start to shroud.
Flowers giggle with a twist,
Nature's humor, can't resist!

A daisy tripped on its own stem,
Told a joke, but who would hem?
Laughter blooms with every breeze,
Even bees just laugh with ease!

Tulips dance in a silly row,
Swaying to the tune of show.
With a wiggle here and there,
They twirl about without a care!

So here's to blooms that joke and play,
In their quirky, flowery way.
Every chuckle in the sun,
Makes the garden more fun!

A Journey in Floral Time

From bud to bloom, a comic tale,
Each flower's face begins to pale.
A sunflower tried to wear a hat,
But bees declared, "That's way too flat!"

Roses blushed, they thought it grand,
To give advice they couldn't stand.
"There's no such thing as too much dye!"
Said the daffodil passing by.

Violets giggle in a choir,
Their jokes spread laughter like wildfire.
With petals wide and faces bright,
They turn the day from dull to light!

Time rolls by, as blossoms sway,
Each laughter helps the worries stray.
So journey forth with blooms so kind,
In every hue, a joy to find!

The Unraveling Mystery

A curious flower asked the sun,
"Do you think I could be fun?"
The sun just winked, "You've got the glow,
Why not dance and steal the show?"

Tulips plotted in a leafy club,
To paint the garden at the pub.
But someone spilled a can of paint,
On daisies, laughing, "Isn't that quaint?"

Rosemary sprigs had jokes to share,
"Why'd the garden philosopher stare?"
"Because he saw a radical stem!
It made him think of a new gem!"

By evening's light, the blooms convene,
To share their secrets, oh so keen.
Through giggles loud and whispers sly,
The mystery blooms beneath the sky!

Echoes of Springtime

In the meadow, blooms unite,
Their laughter fills the morning light.
A dandelion waved a hand,
Said, "Join the fun, it's going grand!"

Buttercups played hide and seek,
While lilacs danced, both shy and sleek.
In every petal, stories weave,
A chorus loud you won't believe!

With honey bees buzzin' away,
They tell of secrets in the fray.
"Why did the lily blush so bright?
Because it couldn't handle the sight!"

So let each bloom bring laughter near,
In every color, joy appears.
Echoes of springtime fill the air,
With every laugh, we show we care!

Each Layer a Story

Each layer unfolds a tale,
Of mischief and of whimsy,
A rabbit thought he'd learned to sail,
But ended up in a frenzy.

With every peel, a giggle's found,
A monkey swung with style,
He slipped on peas that hit the ground,
And wore them like a smile.

The secrets wrapped in leaves so green,
Hold laughter in their fold,
A snail once dressed in glitter sheen,
Got stuck in something bold.

In every crinkle, joys abound,
As creatures dance and sway,
Amidst the blooms, let mirth resound,
And brighten up our day.

Surrendering to the Sun

The sun beams down, a golden tease,
As daisies do a jig,
A crab decided with great ease,
To dance, oh what a sprig!

Clouds laughed loud on cotton candy,
While shadows played a tune,
A squirrel scurried, oh so dandy,
While plotting his balloon.

The daisies turned, their heads so bright,
They flirted with the rays,
A ladybug with spots in flight,
Sang songs of silly ways.

Nature sings in vibrant hues,
In every nook and cranny,
With laughter mixed in fragrant views,
A light heart is our jolly.

The Poetry of Growth

In tiny seeds, a giggle cultivates,
With roots that twist and twirl,
A plant once tried to practice fates,
And stumbled on a whirl.

With sunshine bright and rivers wide,
A veggie wore a hat,
The gopher said, with pride so wide,
"That's quite a fancy brat!"

The flowers hum a jolly tune,
With bees that bop around,
A cabbage swayed beneath the moon,
And lost its leafy crown.

In gardens full of cheerful sights,
With humor in the blend,
Each growth becomes delight, ignites,
Our laughter without end.

Unfurling Dreams

A bud once stretched its arms so wide,
And yawned like it was late,
It tangled up with dreams inside,
And giggled at its fate.

A sunflower had plans to fly,
With petals like a plane,
But tripped and gave the sky a try,
In every twist, a gain.

The wind whispered a secret joke,
As grasshoppers took flight,
While morning glories, woke and woke,
Grew tangled in delight.

Through laughter sprouting everywhere,
In every color scheme,
Life's bloom bursts with joy to share,
A garden full of dream.

Birth of a Silent Symphony

In gardens where the flowers play,
A trumpet blasts, then hides away.
A daisy twirls, a marigold sings,
While the sun just barely brings.

The roses blushed, they thought it grand,
A melody they tried to hand.
But bumblebees stole every show,
Buzzing tunes that just won't slow.

The daisies decided to take a bow,
While violets whispered, "What now?"
A lilac laughed, then slipped in line,
With all their petals, quite divine.

Oh, the hilarity of blooms in chat,
Each flower chirps a little spat.
In silent symphonies, they thrive,
Giving laughs to all alive.

In the Cultivation of Softness

In fields where fluff and giggles roam,
The petals plot to find a home.
They whisper jokes, they tickle the breeze,
Trying to giggle beneath the trees.

A tulip told a joke so bright,
It made the wind laugh with delight.
The daisies clapped, they fluffed with glee,
While buttercups joined in with a plea.

The softest blooms have tales to share,
Of how they twirl without a care.
In sunny patches where they bloom,
They joke about avoiding the broom.

Beneath the sky, they dance and sway,
In the cultivation of their play.
A garden full of laughter's song,
Where softness never feels too wrong.

Fragrant Whispers Unfold

In scents that linger, whispers flow,
Each flower secrets they bestow.
With giggles brewing in the air,
The petals plot a floral affair.

"Oh look!" a rose began to say,
"Let's prank the bees, come on, let's play!"
The lavender chuckled, feeling bold,
"I'll spread the word, let's watch it unfold."

With scents so sweet, a riddle spun,
The jasmine danced, a race begun.
Each bloom with tales of funny sights,
While petals swayed under moonlit lights.

The whispers carried on the breeze,
As flowers snickered with such ease.
In fragrant laughter all around,
Joyful whispers soon abound.

The Language of the Blossom

In petals bright with colors bold,
The blossoms share their tales of old.
They gossip low, in tones so sweet,
While buzzing bees dance to the beat.

A sunflower grinned, all tall and proud,
Telling secrets to the crows, quite loud.
The daisies laughed, they could not hide,
In the language of the flowers, side by side.

Each bloom a character, quirky and spry,
With tales to tell and laughs that fly.
In the garden's grip, hilarity swells,
Among the flowers, all is well.

So if you listen close and clear,
You'll catch their fun in every cheer.
For every blossom has its voice,
In this fragrant world, let's rejoice.

Whispers of Each Bloom

In the garden, blooms start to tease,
They giggle under buzzing bees.
Colors pop like jokes from a clown,
Each wink and flutter, never a frown.

A daisy shouts, 'Look at me sway!'
While tulips dance, 'We're here to play!'
Roses chuckle, a little coy,
Telling tales of garden joy.

The sun beams down with a smirk,
As petals shuffle, they go berserk.
A daffodil slips, trips on a vine,
Sipping dew; oh, how divine!

In this riot of color and cheer,
Who knew flowers could bring such a sneer?
With laughter echoed in soft spring light,
Each bloom a friend, a pure delight.

Gradual Unfolding

A bud peeks out, all shy and sweet,
Wonders when it's time to greet.
With a stretch, it wiggles wide,
A slow reveal; it can't hide!

The leaves laugh, 'Oh, what a sight!'
As more colors join the fight.
'Can I be yellow or maybe red?'
A flower thinks, resting its head.

Each layer pulled back in a blur,
The sun can't stop to purr.
Like a magician, abracadabra,
A burst of brightness; a floral stanza!

As petals flutter and play their tune,
The garden giggles under the moon.
From nervous bud to blooming star,
Who knew flowers could take it so far?

In the Garden of Moments

In a patch of green, laughter blooms,
Nature's jesters break all the glooms.
A winking pansy shares a fun rhyme,
While daisies spin tales of old time.

A sunflower stands tall, making a scene,
Telling the weeds, "You must get clean!"
Chickens and bugs join in the fray,
Tickling the roots, having a play!

'What's the secret?' a bud asks shy,
'To bloom so bright, reach for the sky?'
'Just laugh at the rain and dance in the sun,
Life's a garden, let's have some fun!'

In this patch, time seems to skip,
As bees buzz in for a storytelling trip.
Each moment a palette, colors set free,
In the garden of joy, we just let it be.

Layers of Softness

Softly layered in shades of cheer,
A quiet bouquet whispers, 'Come near!'
Pinks and yellows, a comedy show,
Trading stories only they know.

A tulip jests with petals in a fray,
'Who wore it best?' asks the rose in play.
'It's not the color, but the heart!'
The lilies chime in, playing their part.

Each layer a blanket of giggles and sighs,
Beneath the wide and chuckling skies.
Buds of laughter, trying to grow,
In a world where silliness does overflow.

The garden's secret? It's soft and warm,
Where friendships blossom, free from harm.
With every layer opening wide,
A funny little world where we can abide.

Blossoms in Slow Motion

In the garden, flowers dance,
Caught in a clumsy, silly prance.
Bumblebees trip over their feet,
Nature laughs, oh what a feat!

Tulips twirl like they're on air,
Rosebuds giggle, without a care.
Daisies wink at a passing breeze,
While pansies paint faces with ease.

Colors collide, a riot of hues,
Sunflowers wearing mismatched shoes.
Petals play tag, hide and seek,
Laughter blooms, so unique!

Time slows down, the jokes unfold,
In the garden, stories told.
Nature's humor, a vibrant show,
In slow motion, watch it grow!

Whispers of the Bloom

Whispers float on a fragrant breeze,
Lavenders gossip with such ease.
Chrysanthemums chuckle, humor so sly,
As daisies share secrets with a shy sigh.

Lilies challenge each other to race,
While the wind tries to keep up the pace.
Petal pranks, they laugh out loud,
In this colorful, blooming crowd.

Snapdragons snap, oh what a tease,
While tulips giggle, aiming to please.
A daffodil trips, oh what a sight!
The blooms erupt in pure delight!

Nature's secrets in shades so bright,
Turn the garden into pure fright.
But laughter lingers in every room,
In a world that spun in whispers of bloom!

Fragile Layers Unfold

Layers of laughter, a sight to behold,
With each unfolding, a story retold.
Petals like pancakes, so fluffy and round,
In this playful garden, joy is found.

Daffodils joke, 'Can you hear the buzz?'
While roses reply, 'That's just our fuzz!'
With every layer, the humor grows,
In this patch where giggles and sunshine flows.

Tulips slip on their morning dew,
A slippery dance that's quite the view.
A color explosion, a carnival sight,
When blooms get together, they party all night!

So peel back the laughter, let's see what's there,
In fragile layers, find humor to share.
With every layer that we unfurl,
Life's a riot in this blooming whirl!

Tread Softly on the Softness

Tread softly where the fluffiness lies,
Among flowers wearing bright, cheeky ties.
Each step's a giggle, light as can be,
We're dancing with nature, oh can't you see?

Dreamy petals, a soft parade,
Prancing about without being afraid.
They make a fuss, when visitors come,
'Watch your step! Have some fun!'

Tread lightly, they whisper with glee,
And join in the dance, just you and me.
With blooms all around, the laughter ignites,
As roots start shaking under the lights.

So let's tiptoe through this jovial place,
And find joy in every fuzzy face.
For in this garden with each gentle caress,
We find the softest kind of happiness!

Surrender to the Softness

In the garden where fluffballs play,
Dropping cuddles in a sunny ray,
Fluffy kittens steal the show,
Rolling around like pros in flow.

A dandelion whispers a sneeze,
Tickling noses with the greatest ease,
Laughter dances on breezy air,
While chubby bunnies hop everywhere.

Silly squirrels in acorn hats,
Juggle nuts like acrobats,
Their giggles echo, full of cheer,
As they leap with not a single fear.

Embrace the joy that nature brings,
From happy frogs to silly swings,
Softness wraps the world in glee,
As every bloom sways merrily.

Dreams Wrapped in Color

Rainbows paint the skies so bright,
With candy clouds that dance in flight,
Marshmallow moons hang low and round,
In a world where laughter's found.

Cupcakes frolic on the breeze,
Dancing wildly with such ease,
Jellybeans jump from vine to vine,
In a dreamland, all divine.

With crayon hearts and glitter stars,
Even unicorns drive racecars,
Each color burst a joyful scream,
As we fall into the dream.

The hues of life are sweet and bold,
In every twist, a tale retold,
Wrapped in giggles, soft and bright,
We chase the colors, pure delight.

Echoes of Hidden Beauty

Underneath the leaf-strewn ground,
Whispers of the silly abound,
Giggling worms wiggle with flair,
While beetles dance without a care.

In shadows where the faeries play,
Their tiny shoes go sway, sway, sway,
Blushing flowers give a cheer,
As the mischief draws them near.

A hidden beauty, shy and sweet,
Rides on the breezes, light and fleet,
With tiny giggles, soft and free,
Echoes of bliss are what they be.

To find the charm in what you see,
Is the key to joy; agree?
For in the quirks that life unveils,
Laughter blooms and never fails.

The Unseen Journey of Growth

Once a seed in the backyard's dust,
Dreamed of sprouting; placed its trust,
It giggled as the raindrops fell,
And danced with worms, all is well.

Through dirt and grubs, it had its fun,
While sunlight splashed, it could see the sun,
"Watch me twist!" it shouted loud,
While butterflies gathered, oh so proud.

The roots went deep, but grew so sly,
Wiggling out to kiss the sky,
As petals waved, they laughed and cheered,
The unseen tales from dreams endeared.

With humor stitched in nature's seam,
Every bloom is a joyful dream,
Though hidden journeys go unspun,
They bloom with laughter, every one.

From Bud to Blossom

A bud in a garden, just chillin' out,
Hiding from bees, trying to look about.
With a wiggle and jiggle, it stretches for space,
Wondering when it will win the flower race.

The sun starts to tickle, it giggles with glee,
Wobbling petals like a leaf on the spree.
'I'm a bloom, I'm a bloom!' it starts to declare,
Showing off colors, a floral affair!

But then comes a breeze, and it starts to sway,
Dancing like petals in a bright cabaret.
The butterflies laugh, and the daisies join in,
'Who knew being a flower could be such a win?'

As evening falls down, the bud naps at last,
Dreaming of sunshine and shadows it cast.
'Oh, tomorrow I'll dazzle, just you wait and see,
This flower life is wild, and it's all about me!'

The Art of Becoming

In a world of green, a sprout takes a stand,
Mixing soil and sunlight, it's making a plan.
With dreams of being the life of the show,
It wiggles and giggles, just ready to grow.

A tadpole of green with ambitions so bright,
Wishing for petals that bring pure delight.
It fluffs up its leaves, gets all set to go,
Thinking of ways to impress its flower bro.

Yet in all the thrill of this glorious quest,
The rain clouds roll in, oh, what a jest!
Splish-splashing down, like nature's big prank,
Turning proud blooms into a soggy old bank.

But after the downpour, in the sun's bright light,
Each flower stands tall, oh, what a sight!
In their fanciest colors, with laughter abound,
They strut like the stars of the floral playground!

Soft Hues at Dawn

As dawn gives a wink, the blooms start to yell,
Awake from their dreams in a soft flowery shell.
With colors so pastel, and scents in the air,
They tickle each other in a giggly affair.

A rose shares a secret with a laughing tulip,
'The world is our stage, let's take a big trip!'
They twirl in the sunlight, like kids on a spree,
Who knew morning could bring such a party?

The daisies shout, 'Hey, let's all sway to the beat!'
While the violets hop, their dance moves are sweet.
A daffodil trips, and oh, what a sight,
Is it blossoms or dancers under soft morning light?

So here in the garden, with laughs and with cheer,
Flowers unite like a fun-loving sphere.
Together they'll giggle, they'll bend and they'll grin,
For growing together is the true win-win!

The Quiet Symphony of Growth

In silence they flourish, each budding delight,
A garden of whispers, in morning so bright.
Roots with a riddle, and leaves with a cheer,
Nature's own music, sweet melodies near.

With cells that are dancing and stems that are swaying,
The growth takes a rhythm, a funny ballet.
While shadows play tag and the sun pulls a grin,
A leafy calypso, where laughter begins.

The tulips are singing, a croaky old tune,
As branches join in, they can't help but swoon.
Each bloom has a story, a chuckle, a sway,
Nature orchestrates in her own silly way.

So here's to the journey, where blooms all unite,
In the quiet of growth, there's a weekend delight.
For gardens are treasures filled with joyful mirth,
A symphony played in the heart of the Earth!

Unfolding Dreams in Color

In a garden bright, where giggles grow,
Flowers wear hats, just so they can show.
Bees buzzing tunes, a comical dance,
While worms in the soil plot their next chance.

Raindrops have parties, the leaves are the floor,
They twirl and they spin, never a bore.
A sunflower winks, with a wink it might break,
While daisies tell jokes that make others shake.

The breeze steals a whisper, a laugh in the air,
Butterflies laughing, without a care.
With colors that giggle, the whole garden sings,
A symphony vibrant, with joy it brings.

So come take a stroll, let your smile bloom wide,
In this silly garden, joy cannot hide.
With laughter around, every heart's a performer,
In the circus of colors, life's the true charmer.

A Silent Cradle of Petals

In the hush of the night, where shadows can play,
A flower naps quietly, dreaming away.
The moon casts her smile, a cheeky old friend,
While crickets conspire, with hopes to offend.

A daffodil yawns, with a snore just so loud,
And dandelions giggle, they're quite a proud crowd.
The stars twinkle secrets, so wild and so free,
While night-blooming flowers plot tricks, oh so sneaky!

Leaves rustle softly, like whispers of cheese,
As nature's own jester, the wind starts to tease.
With giggly blooms dreaming of morning's bright stare,
They'll wake with a chuckle, a flamboyant flair.

As dawn peeks with laughter, with sunlight to share,
They'll rise up in colors, no worry or care.
In this silent cradle, dreams dance in delight,
With blooms that are ready to prank the daylight.

The Veil of Natural Grace

In the garden of whimsy, where laughter ignites,
A tulip does ballet, delighting the sights.
The daisies declare it the dance of the day,
While mint leaves toss confetti in a playful display.

Crazy carrots jog laps, they don't want to stout,
And peas have a twerking contest, no doubt.
Roses break out in their glam, look at me!
As the playful parade shimmies, jigs, and is free.

The breeze plays a tune, the flowers all sway,
Sunshine giggles, as it brightens the way.
With butterflies swooping like clowns in a show,
It's nature's own circus, come join in the row!

In this veil of delight, with every bright hue,
Where nature holds court and plays peek-a-boo.
A whimsical waltz amongst blooms in embrace,
Celebrate joy in this funny old place.

Secrets of a Single Stem

Once there was a flower so shy,
Hiding its face in the foliage high.
It whispered tales to bees that flew,
Of awkward dances and breezes too.

With each passing day, it tossed and twirled,
In a game where no one else was twirled.
'Look at me!' it said with a giggle,
But the daisies just wiggled and wiggled.

The ants took notes and scribbled away,
Mapping the sprigs where the flower would sway.
It chuckled loud as it wobbled and spun,
Saying, 'Life is a party—join in the fun!'

Oh, how it danced, that cheeky green stem,
Inviting all critters to join in the gem.
From caterpillars to the whirlybugs too,
It declared, 'Every day can be silly and new!'

The Lull of Hidden Colors

In a quiet garden, colors did play,
But none would peek out on a bright sunny day.
They giggled softly, tucked under leaves,
Whispering secrets that nobody believes.

A violet giggled at the rose in a pout,
'You think you're so pretty, but I'm grand, check me out!'
The rose just rolled eyes with a touch of disdain,
'You might be fun, but I'm bringing the fame!'

Then came the sun with a wink and a grin,
'Why are you hiding? Let's have a win-win!'
But blossoms shivered, too scared to bloom,
As they imagined the fashion faux pas they'd assume.

Finally, a daffodil broke the ice,
'Let's all be silly, there's no need to rise!'
And so the colors burst forth with a cheer,
A fashion parade with no reason to fear!

Growing in Soft Succession

Once in a garden, sprouts lined in a row,
Each eager to show off the skills they could grow.
The basil was first, so fresh and so spry,
While the timid thyme whispered, 'Oh me, oh my!'

They played a game of who could grow tall,
The tallest of plants for the title of 'Small!'
The carrots just chuckled, buried deep in the ground,
Giggles exchanged 'til they tickled the sound.

Suddenly, the pumpkin rolled over with glee,
'Let's grow round and jolly—come join me, pretty pea!'
But the peas just replied, 'We prefer to be sleek,
And fit in our pod—how unique is our streak!'

In the end, all agreed under dainty sky,
That growth is a journey, not just to comply.
So they danced in the soil to the rhythm of rain,
Each sprout sprang to laughter, forgetful of fame!

The Elegance of Layers

Amidst the blooms, there was a grand show,
Layers upon layers, all ready to go.
'I'm the top lady!' said the tulip, so bright,
While petals below giggled, hidden from sight.

A dandelion whispered, 'I'm fluffy and fun!'
But the chrysanthemum scoffed, 'My time has begun!'
'You can't outshine me, not with those puffs,
I've got elegance, layers, and really cool stuff!'

As they argued, the daisies rolled on the floor,
Saying, 'We're just perfect in less than a score!'
Every flower chimed in with a comedic twist,
Layered with laughter, none left out of the list.

And when the breeze blew, all fell in a heap,
Tangled in layers, giggling into sleep.
For flowers know well, in their colorful fray,
Humor is layered, much like they sway!

Beneath the Surface of Bloom

In a garden where daisies feast,
A snail plots a route, to say the least.
With a map made of leaves and a pencil too,
He aims for the rose, but ends in stew.

The bees are buzzing, quite out of line,
Three flowers gossip, sipping on wine.
One flower droops, it's a funny affair,
As it leans on a fence that just isn't there.

A tulip tries wearing a daffodil hat,
But it slips off—oh, imagine that!
The lilies giggle, rolling in glee,
As the garden's a stage for a comedy spree.

Underneath leaves, the worms hold a show,
Telling tales of the dirt, with a grand bow.
It's a circus of roots, all tangled and bright,
Where laughter blooms in the soft morning light.

The Dance of Fragile Whispers

In the twilight, the daisies unwind,
With a twirl and a giggle, so hard to find.
The butterflies cheer, with a flap of their wings,
As the flowers prepare for their zany flings.

A rose took a spin, then stumbled with flair,
Sending pollen flying, oh, everywhere!
The tulips laughed, their colors ablaze,
While the daisies blushed, caught in the daze.

The breeze joined the fun, swirling around,
With whispers of secrets, so silly and profound.
A lilac laughed, 'I've lost my perfume!'
As they danced in the shadows, imagining doom.

With petals a-flutter and laughter so bright,
They twirled on through the soft, starlit night.
In this garden of whimsy, where joy never slips,
Each flower spins tales, on giggling tips.

Slowly Revealing Beauty

A dainty bud woke, feeling quite bold,
Pulled a leaf over, as if to unfold.
It stretched and it yawned, but slipped on the dew,
Tumbling down, what a sight, oh who knew?

The sun peeked in to share the bright news,
It tickled the flowers, giving them views.
But one cheeky bloom, with a smirk on display,
Winked at a ladybug, who danced all day.

The violets whispered, all hopeful and sly,
Waiting for morning, with dreams in the sky.
As hues of the dawn bleached the canvas of night,
The petals all giggled, oh what a sight!

Finally ablaze, they all stopped and stared,
For a swarm of bees buzzed, but really, who cared?
In this slow reveal, where laughter abounds,
Each flower's a joke that joyfully resounds.

To Touch the Tenderness

A soft breeze tosses, the petals all sway,
Each one a slapstick in their own funny play.
With a tickle of sunshine, they sway and they lean,
Creating a scene that's absurdly serene.

The morning glories can't stop their giggles,
As they wag their vines, and do little wriggles.
'Shall we do ballet?' a sunflower teases,
While the pansies blush, caught off guard, oh, geez!

A buttercup trips, but laughs on the way,
As the earthworms cheer for their muddy ballet.
The crickets provide a soundtrack divine,
While the ladybugs chat, sipping nectar from wine.

In this tender embrace, where the wildflowers play,
Nature's laughter echoes in every sweet sway.
Tickled by blooms, let each petal combust,
As we touch the tenderness, relishing trust.

Flickers of Dawn on Blossoms

Morning breaks with giggling blooms,
Tickling the sun with playful plumes.
Butterflies dance in silly jives,
While the sleepy bumblebee strives.

Dewdrops sit like gems on green,
Caught in a game, a sparkling scene.
Nature's laughter fills the air,
As flowers swish with flair to spare.

A daffodil dons a yellow hat,
Waving at bees, 'Hey, how about that?'
Tulips droop, then suddenly spring,
Acting like they own the whole bling!

From roses blush to violets' tease,
They gossip softly on the breeze.
Buds are whispering, "What's the fuss?"
While worms slide by, they must discuss!

The Touch of a Spring Breeze

Breezy whispers tickle trees,
Makes the petals dance with ease.
A dainty flower gives a twirl,
While a daffy lily does a whirl.

Pansies wink, "Hey, look at me!"
"Look how funny we can be!"
Wind rushes in, spills some tea,
And all the leaves shout, "Yippee!"

Dandelions have a wild race,
Blowing seeds in a cloudlike chase.
While tulips strut in colorful rows,
They strike a pose, everybody knows!

An old bee chats with a robin,
Both wondering where spring has gone in.
They giggle at the funny rhyme,
As daisies laugh out loud, sublime!

Gentle Secrets of the Earth

In the soil, secrets hide away,
Earthworms laughing all the day.
Beneath the surface, a party's waged,
With roots dancing, all engaged.

The daisies share tales of last night's rain,
How it tickled and drove them insane.
While mushrooms giggle, "What a sight!"
Spreading whispers of pure delight.

A cricket joins with a cheeky song,
Letting the beetles sing along.
In this hidden, playful zone,
Where the verdant secrets are freely blown.

The ladybugs roll in joyful spins,
Telling stories of where they've been.
With laughter echoing through the ground,
Nature's comedy can always be found!

Layers of Time and Color

Watch the petals, oh what a show,
Layers of color in a vibrant flow.
Each bloom sings with a quirky tone,
Like a painter's palette, all their own.

Tulips throw confetti, red and gold,
While daisies giggle as stories unfold.
A budding rose lets out a snicker,
Spilling secrets, the laughs get thicker.

As time ticks by, the blooms take a bow,
In the garden where antics flow.
Sunflowers chuckle at clouds so shy,
Making funny faces as they drift by.

Every layer hides a little jest,
Nature's humor, surely the best.
With colors blending in a crafty style,
Each flower's grin stretches a mile!

Time's Gentle Unraveling

With each tick of the clock, it seems,
A sock falls from the laundry streams.
Laughter echoes in the hall,
Mom's favorite vase begins to crawl.

The cat dances like it's got flair,
While crumbs from toast float in the air.
We giggle as the clock strikes four,
Just when we thought we'd seen it all before.

The plants lean in for gossip, I'll provide,
With stories of the naps they've spied.
Time's threads unwind with every wink,
Socks in baskets, so much to think!

Yet in this messy, tangled spree,
We find joy in what we can't foresee.
A riddle wrapped in lazy days,
Oh, time, you silly, quirky maze!

The Story Beneath Each Layer

Onions shed their coats with grace,
Every layer has a funny face.
Potatoes tell of muddy quests,
While carrots sport their leafy vests.

In the fridge, the veggies play,
Hiding secrets, come what may.
Cabbages spin tales of the farm,
While broccoli flexes, seeking charm.

Lettuce giggles, full of cheer,
Whispers to the radish near.
With vinaigrette as the gossip queen,
These salads dance in colors green!

So peel away the layers tight,
See the humor in every bite.
There's laughter under each fresh skin,
A crunchy tale where fun begins!

Chasing the Light of Spring

Butterflies flit in midst of cheer,
Wearing glasses, they're party here!
Dandelions puff like little clowns,
As the sunlight chuckles in golden gowns.

The bees use tiny hats for flair,
Buzzing jokes that fill the air.
Hopping bunnies skip and spring,
Singing tunes like it's a fling!

Clouds toss jokes like fluffy balls,
While raindrops bounce off window walls.
In this stage of green delight,
Nature's chuckles take their flight.

So come join this lively ring,
Chasing warmth the springtime brings.
Together in a giggling spree,
Life's a dance, just wait and see!

Beyond the Surface of Bloom

In gardens where the colors clash,
Petunias wear a sassy sash.
Daisies wink at passing bees,
While violets throw a flowery tease.

The tulips gossip, heads held high,
About the clouds that drift on by.
Sunflowers with their sunny grins,
Mimic how the laughter spins.

Behind the blooms, a circus grows,
With ladybugs in tiny shows.
Every stem a funny tale,
In a world where whims prevail.

So peek beneath the fragrant view,
Where giggles bloom and spin anew.
For in this riotous garden play,
Laughter blooms in a bright display!

The Quiet Language of Leaves

In whispers soft, the leaves conspire,
To tell a tale of leafy desire.
They rustle secrets in the breeze,
And chuckle when they tickle trees.

Two squirrels argue, who's the best,
Each claiming acorns, a silent jest.
The branches sway in pure delight,
While birds throw shade in feathered flight.

Harmony in Subtle Hues

Colors clash in nature's style,
Bold and bright, they laugh a while.
A purple bloom with yellow spot,
Jokes about the fashion plot.

Petunias giggle, blush with glee,
As daisies tease from near the tree.
A painter's palette, wild and free,
Nature's jesters in jubilee.

Nature's Layered Lullaby

Underneath the boughs they croon,
Mud pies formed with a sly cartoon.
A snail plays drums on a mushroom cap,
While frogs take turns on a leafy nap.

The wind hums tunes, a haphazard beat,
As worms do the cha-cha 'neath your feet.
Mother Earth joins in with a sigh,
Creating laughter beneath the sky.

The Scent of New Beginnings

Each spring a scent, so fresh and bright,
With flowers scheming to win the fight.
A daisy sways, gets a little bold,
While violets blush, "Don't tell, I'm sold!"

Insects gather, a comical crowd,
Bees gossip loudly, feeling proud.
In whispers sweet, the petals play,
The scent of joy is here to stay.

The Rhythm of Nature's Hand

Leaves do a silly dance,
Wind gives each one a chance.
Flowers giggle in a row,
Buds peek out, say 'Hello!'

Bees wear stripes like a clown,
Buzzing 'round in nature's gown.
Sun's rays tickle every bud,
As worms wiggle in the mud.

Raindrops plop like playful kids,
Making puddles, tossing bids.
Nature laughs, a joyful spree,
Singing tunes, so wild and free.

Trees sway like they know a song,
Swaying happily all day long.
Flowers smile with sheer delight,
In this funny, vibrant light.

Flutter of a Floral Heart

Bees wear helmets, buzzing fast,
In the garden, oh what a blast!
Butterflies play tag with the breeze,
Spinning 'round like clumsy keys.

Dandelions puff like old men,
Waving wild, just now and then.
Tulips burst in colors bright,
Tickling us with sheer delight.

Each blossom turns its head around,
Laughing at the silly sound.
Petunias prance in bright array,
Inviting all to join the play.

Sunflowers nod with winking eyes,
Making all the little flies,
Dance the jig 'neath the sun's glare,
Nature's comedy, beyond compare!

Crescendo of Life

Crickets chirp a funny tune,
Under the light of a round moon.
Flowers yawn and stretch so wide,
Yawning leaves, what a wild ride!

Jesters of the leafy stage,
Bouncing round with perfect gauge.
Each tree wave, a cheeky grin,
Invites all to join within.

Life's a circus, wouldn't you know?
With every bloom, watch the show.
Roses blush, the daisies shout,
What's this joy that they're about?

The laughter swells, the colors rise,
Nature's giggles fill the skies.
In this crescendo, carefree cheer,
Life unfolds, year after year!

A Canvas of Nature

With a splash of yellow here,
And a wink of red so clear.
Nature paints with every hue,
Brushing clouds in skies so blue.

Chubby bunnies hop along,
Nibbling grass, their munching song.
Fluffy clouds float like a dream,
Catching sunbeams' playful gleam.

The brushstrokes of a gentle breeze,
Dancing leaves bring us to knees.
Mischief lurks in every bud,
Bringing smiles, oh what a thud!

Nature laughs in vibrant strokes,
Creating joy with every joke.
A canvas bright with shading fun,
Belting laughter, on the run!

Secrets in a Single Touch

When fingers dance on blooms so bright,
They giggle softly, full of light.
A whisper shared in fragrant air,
With luck they twirl without a care.

Each tap a joke, a laugh, a tease,
A bloom erupts with gentle ease.
The gardener's task, they misdirect,
While blooms conspire to play perfect.

A snicker springs from every bud,
While petals leap and form a flood.
The sunbeam's grin, a wink just right,
Makes flowers chuckle, taking flight.

In nature's jest, they spin and sway,
Each bloom a jester, here to play.
So touch them lightly, let them shine,
And watch their humor intertwine.

Colors in Quiet Softness

In hues so bright, they play their game,
With orange jokes and purple fame.
A pinkish giggle echoes wide,
While yellow blooms burst down the side.

They blush and dazzle, shy yet bold,
In whispers sweet, their stories told.
When colors clash, they start to prance,
In nature's quirky, silly dance.

A palette laughs in softest strokes,
With each new shade, the canvas pokes.
A flower says, "I'm here to cheer!"
Just don't mistake me for a deer.

So if you catch a glimpse of fun,
Know colors frolic in the sun.
In every bloom, a jest does lie,
That makes us laugh, oh me, oh my!

The Hidden Heart of Spring

In spring's embrace, the giggles swell,
As blooms unfold their secrets well.
With every bud that dares to peek,
A joke emerges, softly chic.

The trees conspire with a rustle,
As petals bounce in joyous hustle.
A bouncing bee forgets its aim,
Swapping pollen for a game.

Under the sun, a silly chase,
When flowers beckon, "Come, let's race!"
They play hide-and-seek with the breeze,
Oh, what a laugh in leafy trees.

In hidden hearts where laughter grows,
Springtime's chorus sweetly flows.
With every bloom that grins and sighs,
Nature's jest makes spirits rise.

Threads of Eternal Spring

In woven threads of shiny cheer,
Spring's fabric whispers, "Look right here!"
Dandelions in crazy hats,
Toggle in glee like playful chats.

They stitch up joy in colors bright,
With every bloom, they draft delight.
Silken petals, a flirty waltz,
In stitches taut, no loss, no faults.

A tapestry of vibrant fun,
As laughter weaves through everyone.
With cotton candy clouds up high,
They throw confetti from the sky.

So dance along these threads divine,
In springs eternal, smiles align.
A frolic frame, a bright new start,
With every flower, a funny heart.

In the Arms of the Blossom

A silly bud wears a bright hat,
Dancing around like a jolly cat.
Bees dressed as waiters, serving some dew,
While ants play checkers in dewberry blue.

The breeze starts chuckling, takes off in a spin,
Twirling the petals, let the laughter begin!
A gopher does cartwheels, showing off flair,
While daisies giggle, without a care.

Sunshine spills laughter, brightening the scene,
As flowers gossip on life's silly routine.
Butterflies flutter, teasing each other,
In a garden where joy is like no other.

So let's join the revel, in colors so bold,
Life's too short to be mild and controlled.
With a wink and a bloop, let's laugh till we drop,
In the arms of the blossom, we'll never stop!

Layers of Serenity

Whimsical layers, stacked up just right,
Each one a giggle, each one a sight.
Roses wear socks, lilies wear shoes,
While violets critique the fashion views.

Under the petals, a concert is live,
Crickets in tuxedos, ready to jive.
Bumblebees buzz like they own the place,
Dancing with daisies, a flower parade race.

Sunlight spills laughter, as shadows do play,
Who knew the blooms could party this way?
The breeze tosses confetti, a floral delight,
Joyful and silly, through day and through night.

Let's revel in layers, so vibrant and fun,
In a whimsical garden, where laughter's the run.
Every petal's a giggle, each stem a great tale,
In layers of serenity, we dance without fail!

The Breath of a Flower

With a puff of pink and a tickly sneeze,
A daisy exclaims, "I'm a real tease!"
Sunflowers giggle, tall and stout,
As they pull faces, swirling about.

A tulip tried singing but got a bad note,
So it switched to dancing, and look, it can float!
Petunias are prancing, boots made of mud,
Singing the blues, in a flower-filled flood.

The breath of a flower, whimsical air,
With laughter and joy floating everywhere.
Carnations crack jokes, while lilacs just sigh,
Each bloom has a secret, oh me, oh my!

In this garden of giggles, the fun never ends,
With each little breath, the laughter ascends.
So let's take a moment, enjoy the light show,
In the breath of a flower, let laughter just flow!

The Fragile Dance of Time

Tick-tock on the petals, the clock starts to sway,
A flower says, "Come on, let's dance today!"
With giggling stems and a bouncy bouquet,
They twirl in the breeze, come what may.

Butterflies flit, with a wink and a grin,
Challenging daisies, "Can you keep up, kin?"
A blossom, quite luscious, starts popping some moves,
In a fragile dance, everyone grooves.

Time flutters by, holding on to a laugh,
As shadows sway gently, in nature's own half.
With petals that jiggle, and buds that play pranks,
In this garden of joy, we pull all the ranks.

So let's take a snapshot, of fun on the vine,
In the fragile dance, we'll sip on some wine.
Celebrate each moment, let giggles entwine,
For time's just a whisper, as we sip and dine!

www.ingramcontent.com/pod-product-compliance
Lightning Source LLC
Chambersburg PA
CBHW070317120526
44590CB00017B/2714